ROUGH, AND SAVAGE

ROUGH, AND SAVAGE

POEMS

SUN YUNG SHIN 신 선 영

COFFEE HOUSE PRESS

Minneapolis 2012

Coffee House Press books are available to the trade through our primary distributor, Consortium Book Sales & Distribution, cbsd.com. For personal orders, catalogs, or other information, write to: Coffee House Press, 79 Thirteenth Avenue NE, Suite 110, Minneapolis, MN 55413.

Coffee House Press is a nonprofit literary publishing house. Support from private foundations, corporate giving programs, government programs, and generous individuals helps make the publication of our books possible. We gratefully acknowledge their support in detail in the back of this book.

Good books are brewing at coffeehousepress.org

LIBRARY OF CONGRESS CATALOGING-IN-PUBLICATION DATA
Shin, Sun Yung.
Rough, and savage : poems / by Sun Yung Shin.
p. cm.
ISBN 978-1-56689-314-5 (alk. paper)
I. Title.
PS3619.H575R68 2012
811'.6—DC23
2011046605

PRINTED IN THE UNITED STATES
1 3 5 7 9 8 6 4 2
FIRST EDITION | FIRST PRINTING

For Jae and Ty

and so I stoppped, bewildered, I believe

sand kindled like tinder under flint

loom, spindle and thimble for the telling of fortunes

their strange laments beset me, each an arrow

so thick a veil above its currents as this

who pierces the world

Nel mezzo del cammin di nostra vita
mi ritrovai per una selva oscura,
ché la diritta via era smarrita.

Ahi quanto a dir qual era è cosa dura
esta selva selvaggia e aspra e forte
che nel pensier rinova la paura!

To tell

About those woods is hard—so tangled and rough

And savage

—DANTE ALIGHIERI (1265–1321), *The Inferno,*
VERSE TRANSLATION BY ROBERT PINSKY

BEGGAR } CHOOSER { BEGGAR

Was the first to cross over a woman, curious, or alone

Gift of a stone axe, a stone net sinker:

(bones found at both sites, Paleolithic remains)

THE EXCHANGE OF A CHILD
THE GIFT OF A CHILD

A child lost on the way to gather (fire) became distracted by a moving stripe
He follows the snake through broken leaves

Clouds whiten the transaction

Metal arrives heavy from the north, tin and copper

Sword and shield—
now arm the future

The Dream of Bronze-Age Man:

I am a son of heaven. Let my dolmen break
the horizon with its back of bone, stone
shoulders and a door like no other

My body, my bronze, my tribe—written with
an axe that mocks the curve of the moon

Night tumbles over herself to sleep in my
armor.

Night stains me with power and I grow a shell
made of metal

I will live yet tomorrow to eat this wealth
from the dirt-black hands of my brother

I am a son of heaven.
It is proclaimed

My Father, my fever, our will is as one.
I will talk in this metal, and hammer out your
command

Bury me, here, in this endless favor

If they can speak within those sparks of flame

Time grows a serpent's tail, scales multiply, petrified, can be crushed between teeth, ground to powder, swallowed and kept.

MAN, THE INVENTIONIST
to be sown
to be born, squall and steam, blind and mewling
to break branch
to eat root
to split seed
the flesh of fruit, red and ruin

< TERRITORIUM > the place where people are warned off
circle
> excess, surplus, reserve

circle

(to protect what is yours)

On a bleached island

A plague upon the city

She, the sphinx, laid out a riddle like a river of fire

What walks on three legs in the evening

> excess, surplus, reserve

When the creature throws herself off a cliff
The curse is lifted like the canopy of night

The hero returns, fatherless, motherless

Death is vanquished, death turns from itself, death eats
its own name

"I am the future. I and my descendants," he cries.

The crown. The sun. The circle closes.

                         Man assumes the throne.

     Three-personed God, go back. Go back through this frozen land
of dust and shadow.

> excess, survival, repetition, ritual, ceremony

Art. Again. All that is beauty and terror shall be carved in stone,
poured in gleaming metal.

                A volcano within the heart, its lakes of fire.

        Hold your hands just so.
        Hold the fire this way.
        Cast the light on her face, but not hers.

        Throw the robe over that child, not the other.

Bind and abandon that one—the prophecy is upon its heart like a foreign coin.

Gold and copper.

> Step heavy into this floating bark.
> A footfall like lead.
> A beating heart draws the damned.

When the first human fashioned a box, we began to conceal things from one another. To hoard meant to survive.

Work at this riddle as though walking backward up the stairs.

The cocoon unknits itself, silk falling to threads.

You are a child again.

Something alights on your shoulder—
a sparrow, a firefly, the hand of your brother, nearly identical to your own.

Crimes have yet to be committed

Punishment has yet to be invented

*No sooner were all things separated in this
    way,   confined*
            stars   buried
in darkness and obscurity,   blaze
       forth

—OVID, A REDACTION FROM *Metamorphoses,*
TRANSLATION BY MARY M. INNES

all the world's cravings

—DANTE ALIGHIERI, *The Inferno,* Canto I

| | | Neither iron scissors nor wee coat turned inside out could divert me. Their threads beckoned to my teeth. The seams rhymed with the fault lines of the body. *Changeling,* I heard. | | |

| | | I made a replacement child of plant matter, of stone, a stock, an enchanted block of wood. It soon grew sick and died, fooling no one but the country doctor. His leech jar and black bag. His fingers steepling and unsteepling. His brother the priest came with oil, water, and smoke. | | |

| | | I flew from monsoon to dams of stick and mud, ash and aspen, birch and fir, oak and elm and silver maple. I sliced the great wood myself with spinning metal wheels. | | |

| | | I lived in one box, then another. I carried my shell with me like a nautilus, growing larger with every home, filling the air around me with patterns and polish. | | |

| | | I worshiped their God inside marble cracked open like an egg. Veined with God, streaked with God. I ate him and caught his blood in my throat. He tasted like innocence and I came to crave his flesh. I became a virgin again and again. | | |

| | | To the nave, I was taken to count coins, light candles in my devotion to the spirits departed. My namesake, my un-naming. | | |

| | | Never did I view a dead body until it was anointed, emptied. Something written on the face, but blurred. I buried no one with my own hands. I buried my hands and was the handless maiden. My hands were strapped to my back. I was pitied. I was given silver hands by my king and dropped our baby in the water. | | |

| | | The tinsmith made a new voice for the witch who ate my mother. Then she spoke with the flavor of her voice, it was like a funnel calling me. | | |

| | | I was taken to the tomb to fold the flag of my forefather. | | |

| | | I became my enemy, iron. When no one was looking I swallowed a wedding ring and separated gold from silver, bright from base, sin from sinner. I was a panning in their river, heavy metals sank in me. | | |

| | | I obliged my country like a serving girl. I learned to spell and love the spelling, the uttering of our symbols. Pictographs rubbed off the walls onto my skin, turning me ochre and wild with a dress printed with arrows and spears. | | |

| | | Animal skin dressed my feet, waist, and even my own hands. I became the animals I ate until I stopped eating them. They were to live outside my body but on my body where I could watch them. Tongueless they could no longer talk to me, give me news. I shed vegetable matter and the cells from inside my body. I was never clean. | | |

| | | I swallowed sorrow with my porridge and memory with my dinner roast. I devoured my terrible mother straight from the oven. I chopped wood, my brother, I filled my dipper with water, my sister. I forgot my father and his worries. | | |

| | | Still, I was not returned. Still, the human child walked over my paths, following deer and moonlight. It knew nothing of devilry. An isomorph. It refused to age though I grew bent and withered. | | |

| | | Bewildered, without words or wisdom, a thimble in its pocket, it wades deep into the babbling river, water snakes like black ribbons round its ankles, a silver flash of fin, a passing thought, always my eyes upon its mute, unchanging figure—

KINGDOM OF THE LIGHT, KINGDOM OF THE DARK
(A MONOLOGUE IN SEVEN PARTS)

SATAN THE WANDERER:

I place my self in the palm of my hand

I lie against the bent fingers

as in an oyster shell, a bit of grit, a child-sized swallow of nacre

No-color

                                      My throat in tatters—was it lions? was
it you?

                              unwrapped like a gift or an afterthought

It closes and I have forgotten the gnashing of teeth

        Nothing can keep me from healing; I am sealed like wax

And G-d asks unceasingly this question

        From whence have you come

                    My ears suffer his voice

My tongue suffers his taste

G-d speaks but I am a writer

Only I can mark time with my fingers around this bit of black

I fold perfection into these spindles, ink

The alpha and beta: now I am Greek, now I am Hebrew

What are these dark marks across the cheek of this page but stains

the sailing of my foot across a great face

a smear, a grin

G-d makes predictions and I scratch in the sand and dirt

Never does he utter the word *son,* or *daughter*

His breath is my only cloak; see how it stirs

My answer trails behind me, moving as I do, quickly now, quickly, naked, unseen, not even the air moving around me

I smell nothing like an animal, you cannot bird or beast me

Like wings my answer unfolds, feathered and pierced

From wandering the earth and walking on it
From wandering the earth and walking on it
From wandering the earth and walking on it

THE GIFT, THE ENVY:

What do I need to do to seduce you
        other than be invisible as I am?

        Let me in

The cry of the child who lives in the morning, now

        Let me in

The midwife packing boiled cloth between your legs

        Let me in

The bloody water burning through snow

        Let me follow your sight though I am unseen

        Let me follow you like your own envy

THE WATCHER:

The little match girl's limbs are like spindles

       I turn them in my hands for heat that never arrives

Call me to your banquet, young one

Sing me closer, sing me sewn into your pocket

THE SLANDERER:

My name itself means "accuser." To be hostile, to hate, to be hated—

Yet I know your afflictions and your poverty. What shall be the utterance of the day, what circus of calumny, what storm of defamation may I bring to you?

> *Listen my beloved brethren, were you not born to be poor?*

> Cast aside your riches

> Cast aside your possessing of all things

> Cast aside thy burdens and teachings, all that lie heavy
in the mouth

THE SCAPEGOAT:

I will drive you into the wilderness

Un-inhabit me / your fingernails horned and rifled like a seashell

                              Smitten
                              Stricken
                              Afflicted

    "The goal shall bear upon you this face through the fog of atonement"

                              Azazel, my cliff, my Christ

My pharmakos, my famine—

                    I wandered lonely as a cloud

                              my last hot meal was a stone full of rain

ASTRAY, FUGITIVE:

On my knees, plates and shanks of bone
pushing outward until my skin is white,

red, scraping the dirt, pebbles in flesh

Live here—at this carnival, to see you in the unfolding of mirrors

In truth—there are no horns, tail, virgins,

wives. No black-lapped coven, hair thick with the scent of
broken pine needles

I blushed once, then never again
My blood was borne away for other uses

A bloom, a blossom, snow white and rose red

Can I be the daughter and the tiger at the door?

The great chuffing bear at the stream and the steel-colored glint of evening

If I had a fur coat like his I would eat the rust from your body, coin you and spend

you at every revelry

my name—never painted, never rustic
on the signs of the traveling sideshow

This is dust, a gluttony of amusement

I, at last, am raising flesh

THE ARTIST:

It is I, not He, the one who draws your bath, separates the steam from the heavy rope of water—

How do you record the con perpetrated upon us all? We, the lesser?

> I trained as an astronomer when the earth was a flat dish of dirt, when it was drowning in sand.

> None of us can eat glass, not even I, but I make the gesture

Here with you, in your embrace, armed resistance, stand, prison, my house

> Our child, our child, the future opens like a night flower

> Its perfume makes me forget, makes me cry out

> I am broken across the body of the earth

> Rock and willow, a thing green

> Everything I make is unmade, a bed in the morning, your memory of me—

churned in my heart's lake
all through the night

—Dante Alighieri, *The Inferno,* Canto I

^ ^ ^

This concavity, the blood to pool and wait
                                        In the end
                    Made of wood and fever and fear
Below a hill that marked one end of the valley
            lay many landed boats waiting
            to be weighed and measured
                                smoked and swallowed

the rectangular word *coffin* with its double gallows between "co" and "in"
                                        but meaning nothing like *go in*
            sheared stumps of oak trees, coarse platters, gravestones floating on grass

                                    To plunge underground
            a bank of mahogany marks a watery profile
                        Uneven locket
                                            hinge, jaw

^ ^ ^

I wanted everything about me to outlive me

I want to leave threads on the ground so I might return
               without the pinch and itch of memory

                 At night a great watch becomes a cuff of sand
       and we wake with the taste of grit and glass

Knife
       cut my necklace
Flame
       melt the clasp and its miniature hands

^ ^ ^

We were poor students to have never learned the names of things
                I cry because I was not Adamic
                    All specificities coalesce into the purity of icon
waxen, graven, ivory, gold
                Isis and Osiris
                    at the end we each become the throne

    Memory: My shadow was a thief, a hoarder of regret, the sly one

    I am weak now, deposed and in plain sight
arranging my gold rings upon my tongue

                Diamonds roll over the range of my knuckles
    remembering the anguish of compression
                          and being cut for fire

∧ ∧ ∧

Here I am, in a state

of starvation for metaphor, famished for a comparison

of one thing to another, even the various taste of trash

Even *thing* sounds like metal

the song of it turning my skull into a stainless cup

I change sizes with each breath

David and Goliath

soldier and enemy

son and sister

A list

I lie as in a loop

I renew my distant colonies

I forget how to avenge myself

∧ ∧ ∧

Death, you're my owl, my nightingale, my wren—
You may sit in my branches as long as you like.
I will watch with gladness as you play
our hunting game with the last grasshopper

all other loves are masks for these

—ROBERT PINSKY, *The Inferno,* introduction to his verse translation

Country of the sick, pilgrim and poet
Through the glass, through the mask
God-sculpture, between us, bowl
Pour our love, wash our love, sift
The impurities, stains of love

Golden bowl, common gourd, gold and steel
Base metal, tin, soldier, beggar
Our god, ikon, camera, no-time
Inner eye, made of time, opposite
Silent eye, grain of light

Radiant, a robe, white alphabet
The love of self, secret room
City of Man, building, brown brick
Hand and trowel, here, heavy
Inside, little room, table made of flesh

Twelve heads, mouth to eat air
Hand, longs for its mirror-mate
Rings and collars
Hell, the earthly city an encampment
Autonomous world, limit situation

Infants turn, faces, any face
A crudely drawn face on any piece of paper
Which boat to choose
Which foot to fall first
When to set sail

What silver to sew into the lining
Single bowl, saline current, the Under-River
Pilgrim, poet, professions
Wash through this love, rock and blade
Beds of down, beds of earth

BEST PROTECT: CLIPPINGS

my *beautiful* [war] fair box-and-circle

                steel dial, stainless [body] numbers

       a clock-face to keep [my baby] clean

     a ribbon of time unfurls one way

                "on what you build not what you destroy"

            gentle, cycle

hands to bake and [bomb and] burn [and vanish]

          a sharp, wooden toothpick pulled [and put back in]

[my *beautiful* white enamel]
lost tooth [child] in a box, dark cake of earth to hail him
under his pillow, root & nerve

that was [my *beautiful*] operation

once [the Blue Fairy in that movie about
the timber boy who dreamed of the real]

[the] "Mother!" [of all Battles] *the babe cried from his cradle*

my beautiful [metal] face [lies] like a Roman
mask lit with a candle made from animal fat

"No-one" [can be pleased] can be designed [to best protect]
invite me to do what you would have us do—

away from here and through an eternal place

—Dante Alighieri, *The Inferno,* Canto I

우리나라 ★ URI NARA ★ [OUR LAND]

I.

Contemplate the meaning of aperture, of distance.

    A pinhole camera and the silk-thin screen—

II.

For us, there is a typical exposure time.

    "You put your F-stop in my solar eclipse."

III.

A hand-operated flap; black wings of a headless bird

    one eye one hundred times smaller than the distance to the surface of the
camera

IV.

My baby, my body, my belly, my royal jelly!

    Who is this *obscura,* this *dark chamber.* Why should I be denied the flesh?

V.

"The depth of field is basically infinite."

    Our images have been inverted—I could love indefinitely like this—

VI.

F-stop. delivery. stop. stork. stop. shower. stop. clean. stop. banish filth. stop.

    If a daughter chewed on this sewing needle could she make a dress out
of her face?

VII.

OUR LAND, our gang, our stand, our hands, our five-hundred-year-old hojuk.
   What of the world written in the private, dark white ink of men's bodies?

VIII.

I always hated the sound a _____ makes while slapping me for being too historical.

IX.

Now we have a permanent blush, the flame of health.

X.

The number ten is the edge of a cliff. A line and a hole.
   This country and its negative print, a silver face through the fog, a certain
   development—

therefore if you escape from this dark sphere

—Dante Alighieri, *The Inferno,* Canto XVI

Korean state   existed
several millennia

until the 20th century, Korea existed
Chinese tributary state

at the conclusion   War
Treaty   Imperial Japan
War   Korea   Treaty.   Tokyo annexed the
Peninsula   independence   surrender   United
States in 1945.   World War II,
southern half   Peninsula   government
north   War   US troops
UN forces   soldiers
attacks   China   Soviet Union   armistice
splitting   demilitarized zone
regime   rapid eco-
nomic growth

first civilian president
years of military rule   fully functioning modern democ-
racy   global engagement

Nuclear Security Summit
Serious tensions   punctuated
sinking   warship Cheonan
artillery attack   soldiers   citizens

59

REDACTION: UNITED STATES CENTRAL INTELLIGENCE AGENCY | THE WORLD FACTBOOK | EAST & SOUTHEAST ASIA :: KOREA, NORTH

kingdom long history occupied Japan

War later formally

entire World War II split

control failing

War conquer US-backed

founder

"self-reliance"

outside influence demonized ultimate

threat propaganda

core ideological objective

unification control.

successor

death

power mismanagement

misallocation

aid feed military

provocations long-range missile

nuclear devices massive

conventional armed forces

regime 2012 centenary birth banner year

improving

people's livelihoods.

(RIOT POLICE)

This is you—Titanus giganteus, your maw snapping pencils in half and
cutting through human flesh. My encyclopedia chokes on your bulk.
My camera, timid, afraid to look, as if you're naked—not one adult
male, but millions.

Few garments sound as fine as *flak jacket,* the best of the tagmata the tho-
rax, more prime than brains as the body can keep mating, cracking its
margins. Your shield like a wing, protects your bulletproof heart from
the wind, your right arm black in the cloth of your brothers. Full face
visor. Baby gladiator.

Beyond the screen, memorized—jawbone like a scandal reflecting all
the thieves and beggars. Insect lord, insect mind. This is my fear. You
look like my brother, my son. You could kill me with your looks.

(PYONGTAEK, U.S. MILITARY BASE EXPANSION)

A white neocolonial house looks out onto the fields, limbless, no fingers to flute the rice, green and young. The sun like a pendant on a woman's neck, hanging above a fine gown.

They're wearing identical white raincoats, or nearly white, like hulled rice, which, if you hold it up to the light, shows a touch of translucence. They can't win this though they lick the chain-link wallpaper until their tongues grow rough as a cat's. The farmland already history, a museum, a field of graves. Future crop nothing but soldiers.

Too much salt in the soil, weeds, and blood. A knife plunged into rind. Split open the second pumpkin, wicked brother, though the first yielded a host of goblins drunk on your misfortune. You are what you are.

You never said you loved this. Money-takers and flames, your manor blackened to ash—yet still you kiss the bird's broken leg.

(NAJU, WEEDING AT THE BASE OF THE PEAR TREE)

A black snake, ringed green, almost slashed by the scythe, the shaft called the snath, the slight curve of the blade, perpendicular to the grasping hand, torso parallel to the trunk.

Heel, touch the ground, kiss the grass, grate against the brunette bark of the tree, its arms hung with ivory bags like lanterns, wrinkled like pillowcases around the light, the fruit, forbidden until they break, split paper like a back beneath an old work shirt.

The hand, rust and sweat—now, sharpen, peening the edge, a whetstone. On the dirt, a pile of letters, the sound *kah* or *gah*. Drink and keep downing the day. The snake—good for liquor—curled smooth in a tree like a question mark.

(DEMILITARIZED ZONE)

Like a wedding ring, or the bride's green ribbon, you shelter me.
No business but war. You remind me of a kind of heaven.

A cairn of rocks casting shadows in the shape of a man.

Thou art the table before me in the sight of my adversaries, thou dost
anoint my head: oil and rain, thou art a ghost with a girl's mouth,
thou art not the making of my dreams—under water, under cliff,
under this long suitcase of earth and bombs. More than any mortal
could gather beneath the skirt of the sky.

You are never eager, nor famished, nor pale with a craving for white
clothes or my nocturnes.

Let your lynx approach, even tiger, even its wild outline.

You need no ferryman or the obolus of the dead.
If I put a coin in my mouth I taste copper, not the corpse.
They say that bodies fertilized the ground so well the trees grow
bright and tall. The bones blur. We return alive.

(MOUNTAIN, JIRISAN NATIONAL PARK)

Gifts crept to us and I made a crown of your mushrooms, a cape of fat slugs, a veil of spiders.

With each mouth-sound we stitched our skin to the face of the water, we made a blind, a blanket out of the backs of girls, black hair feathering the waves.

Here is where the maidens faded down from heaven, the hem of their dresses curtained the face of the hunter, the rag at his table, the sweep of his childlessness. It smells of mineral and leaf, of spiky puffs—bombs of seeds or the pine's punctuation.

Here, nothing fits to a man's hand but her, the youngest, fine to be first and last, least seen, the most to see.

(THE NORTH KOREAN OBSERVATORY) A FAUX-KU

The shoes of North Koreans sit patiently behind the vitrine, as if outside a neighbor's door.

North Korean money fingers itself soft like flannel.

Ginseng wine sings its sour ballad, while I slide my wŏn into the binoculars' sly slot-mouth.

(OUTSIDE THE GATE AT CAMP HUMPHREYS, U.S. MILITARY BASE)

That tank is my wet nurse, my elephant mother, my protector and avenger. That soldier in pixels was the star of my video game last night. The sheets were wet with sweat—*I want to win.* I play in bed because there I can see all of you.

He wears my face during the day, camouflaged, goggles and compass, my hair between his teeth. I worry, worry. I sleep in his mouth. I am liquor and gag.

(BUDAE CHIGAE / "GARBAGE" STEW NEAR THE PROSTITUTION CAMPTOWN)

"You'll be taken first."   (This girl is a classic beauty.)
"And you look like a minister."   (This man has a kind face.)
"You look like a fox."   (I am a female ghost, a demon.)

Laughter—gold chain and cigarette.

At least I am not the egg ghost, the woman who wears a blank face.

At least I am not the maiden, buried before she could become a woman.

At least I am not the bone who was the maiden, waiting to be shown his finest treasure.

To be pissed on, to be brought to life. This folktale.

The steam cleans my fox face. The stew smells like ham, hemul, and a boy's salt-stained neck.

and so I stoppped, bewildered, I believe

—DANTE ALIGHIERI, *The Inferno,* Canto XIII

IT IS AS A PEASANT TO TIME THAT I ENTER THIS DREAM

THIS GILDED PALACE AND THIS FISHING NET

become the memorant with me

BRING ACROSS THE SEA WHAT I HAVE FORGOTTEN

CARTOGRAPHY THE WAR ROOM THE MARCH OF CIVILIZATION

MY MOST IMPERFECT KNOWLEDGE: THE 1816 VOYAGES OF THE *ALCESTE* AND *LYRA*

Despite the survey work

Count and map me—my islands

My shores a terror to mariners.

what native map of recent days

and yellow sky. Resort of the

Teal, crane, curlew, quail.

Gaudy with beauty the likes of

Even the coast shoals of whales—

Shipwreck the stranger devils,

sail and

lay me down like a book, bound.

and archipelagoes, shoals and reefs.

My most imperfect knowledge—

and spacious harbors. Green sea

sea-fowl and fisherfolk, my lonely home.

Tiger lilies, daisies, asters, cactus, ferns.

which I've never seen. Snow-white herons.

to black ships and fickle fate.

dangerous generosity of south

passing flame.

SEOUL, DECEMBER 1883

A handkerchief fluttered, thrust through iron bars, shuttered loophole windows well nigh brushed in passing.

Too fitting a fancy to be fulfilled.

Percival Lowell and his Japanese secretary had dinner with the Japanese Consul. Japanese was his stepmother tongue. The palanquin ride followed from coast to capital.

Acute remembrances.

Constrain me, poverty, so that I may amplify the day's march to two.

Assert yourself, romance. Rise, city, rise.

The compound, the party walls, the gates, and sittings—here the Foreign Office, here the gaily uniformed escort!

It was virgin. It was tigers and leopards. It was cut-off cousins and stuffed with chestnuts.

Drunk, flush on the rosy tints of the wine-dark dying day.

"Since the days they feasted me almost all my Korean official friends have met violent deaths. Even as I write, Korea has ceased to exist."

1895, THE KING OF KOREA IS A VASSAL OF CHINA

History to be found, Teacher Cloud
The land like a dress it closed around me
Violent sleep, the serpent's yawn and swallow
Tail like a whip it shone as a gem

ONE ∞ TREATY ∞ KINGDOM ∞ TENANT ∞ ONE

"The path of progress, my liege lord"
"All this time China had been in intercourse with foreigners"

Confession, Teacher, eggs eaten and all
Skin, her skin, shell, her shell
Scales, this page cracked and white
Lip bit, blood apostrophe

SALT ∞ STOP ∞ SENTENCE ∞ DEER ∞ PRESERVE ∞ WINTER

When we hunt we set aside the heart, the liver, the starry crown.
Fealty, even love

The word *politics* begins with a kiss and ends with a hiss.

COAL AND IRON AND GOLD

"Indeed the nation is without ambition."
A measure of ruins and reforms on each broken nail, a wheel of horn, a trial of transition.

She is sewn up with railways and telegraphs, black stitches and an iron smile. Her hospitality—we must bend under the wire.

My face a vast blank, a half-savage nomad, I admit, I admire my advance.
Foreign trade the name Hermit Kingdom.

No hermit, no king. Goldmines and cigarette factories.
Stop your sentimental facial resemblance to the Caucasian race.

AMERICAN MISSIONARY

I am a union of devices. My fruit farm, my zeal.

Carve me from labor.

I will smooth the brow of any convert. My thumb fears no flesh!

I am her husband, I am his wife. I am their large and luxurious children, flinging themselves through the blue on the seesaw. Her very bare feet, my woman, my wife. The white feet and inside her white bones.

At night her body makes a white cross against the sheets. Star liquor and the red scent of freckles.

Nothing creeps under our door to paint its headlights across the headboard. No natives. No verse. No Latin!

No traffic but the blank heat of my prayer, tracing the white cross, bone against bone.

My appeal, my plea, my application of restraint.

FORESIGHT, AUGUST 1910

Rain began in between the infinity.
There was Russia and Japan.

Survey what holds the wings together, the lobes of the butterfly.
Like lanterns, like lungfish.

A firm foothold for American commerce, says Charles Welsh, "a party
of peaceful but powerful expansion has prevailed."

Compel me to quote these forefathers—their flocks and fisheries
went unfathomed by me in 1883.

I was there, I was there, I was seldom visited by travelers.

He and he and he called me mainland, he called me daughter, he
pressed his unfolding bodies upon my fortification.

sand kindled like tinder under flint

—DANTE ALIGHIERI, *The Inferno,* Canto XIV

ISOLETTE

1.

I reached into the isolette and turned the baby on its side, gently but firmly like turning a breakfast sausage link, as to keep the browning even.

2.

The baby did not protest, but it did turn its twin black eyes at me and blink, like the animal it was. I blinked back. I felt something tender pulse to life within me. It was as though a little glass opened up a space in time, a little circle of memory, a little round of moonlight. Old-fashioned Korean combs are round, or at least I think they are, and I longed to hold one in my palm, its even teeth making a series of small red dots, a temporary score.

3.

There was a visitor, a priest, or a cleric of some sort. Unfortunately, he smelled dank and old. The skin on his cheeks was mottled like a toad, and somehow shiny as though worn down, down, down. There was hair in his ears and it was black, but his eyebrows were white. He looked like some kind of forest animal. I glanced at his greasy black cuffs and half expected to see broken branches and rusty leaves issuing forth, competing for space with his bony yellow wrists.

4.

We talked about clouds, about how they were simultaneously worldly and ethereal, an illusion, heaven made of water droplets and dust particles. How we saw our futures and our pasts in them, but never our present. He said, "The term I use for a cloud's appeal is *eidetic charisma*." At this utterance, the baby blinked, twice, and began to cry. Its toothless, dark mouth was the size of my question and just as unanswerable.

5.

"I love that term. Here, let me write that down." I reached for a plain ballpoint pen, its end chewed to wet feathers, and a sheet of lined paper. EIDECTIT—

"No, that's not it! You're missing a *c,* and you have an extra *t.*"

EIDECTIT—

"No! You're not listening!"

"Spell it for me again, slowly."

"E – I – D,"

As I wrote down the letters they began to change. When I looked down at the paper again, they had multiplied, and rearranged themselves into something like this:

carneaform andelentearnicon deaquisticonuis

I bent to write and long drops of black ink splashed onto the paper. I shook the pen, hard. On the page, shapes began to form. Clouds, no, horses. Four spotted horses, running. I looked up at the priest (or cleric). The baby had stopped crying and was chewing a corner of its blanket.

6.

I noticed that the blanket, a cheap affair more like a cotton kitchen towel than a blanket, was printed with pastel hot air balloons. This same blanket, or its copy, or its cousin, was the same that the American hospitals wrapped around my own children after their births, washings, weightings, and scorings. I thought then, as I did here, that hot air balloons were a poor choice for something so newly subject to the laws of gravity, and ordinary oxygen, and falling.

7.

The man was gone. I turned the baby on its back, to look at the crack in the ceiling, and I ran after him.

8.

There is more to the dream, but it involves the odor of smoke, and tiny white worms swimming through the carpet at the orphanage (or the primary school). It involves children upturning their plastic lunch trays and a nun, the receptionist, shaking in anger.

9.

I went back to the baby, of course.

10.

Her eyes were dry, and bright, and she didn't seem to mind the irony of the hot air balloons on her towel-blanket. Her forehead seemed to show no memory of the priest-cleric, no troubles creased her little yellow-pink brow. She had a little constellation of milia on her nose, that was all. I put my little finger into her hand and she grabbed it, and held on tight.

11.

The Korean orphanage worker swept by and said something in Korean that sounded like a question. I noticed her slim ankles and flat black shoes. She left no footprints on the hard white floor. My own shoes were chunky and seemed foreign, though they were made in China.

12.

I leaned down to the baby and had the urge to bite her, but instead I gave her the smallest kiss. I combed her tuft of black hair with my fingers and pinched her tiny ear, just a little edible mushroom, and left my mark, if only for a moment.

13.

The sound of horses or the odor of clouds—

FORMER COMFORT WOMEN NOT ALLOWED BY THE KOREAN POLICE IN FRONT OF THE JAPANESE EMBASSY IN SEOUL

goose-legs of the folding chairs, the dark fluttery triangle
of my fan, the heated air folding back
mourning, younger sister,
nearly my age, always the same distance

*

all things will outlast this: "can I take your
oral history?" she says, just a girl—
(what can I take?)

AUGUST 1950, 8,000 KOREAN REPLACEMENTS

A louse crawled from the new soldier's scalp.

In a dream, the louse was my brother. Hundreds of us turned to grass
and began carpeting the man's body, wrapping it in a fine green field.

The army photographer raised his camera but the machine browned
and soured like a rotten apple. Its dull black skin shriveled in his grip.
His tripod became a three-legged deer and sprinted across enemy lines.

*loom, spindle and thimble for
the telling of fortunes*

—Dante Alighieri, *The Inferno,* Canto cxx

AVAILABLE

There were too many women
and children for the wind to eat.
A cottage industry without the cottage.
From under bridge to skyscraper. Wayfarers,

call us sentimental, but we prefer
crow over raven, pigeon to dove.

DAUGHTER AT THE MUSIC STAND

Minuet in G—the virgin energy
of the strings under chin:
Child of my marriage, future of my
patient, past childhood. You shed me, stretch my skin

Metronome in its black case, "Never let me go, never
let me go—"

ACQUISITION

The portmanteau, mouth wide as its body
to carry the basic written symbols—
caught in ghastly tinny teeth
of zippers, descent in pockets, conceal and swallow

The language learner, unbuckle, shine mirror, doubling
paper, all the day's news, back and now

RETURN OF THE NATIVE

Because of time being an arrow, I had to imagine everything.

I had to fold the song with my mind because of the time being. Wash
the rice here, in the present.

Because of the arrow I pent up the fourth wall as though I were dia-
pering my own newborn.

I put time to the breast, though I feared it was not an arrow but an asp.

Being time I kept that fear under my tongue like a thermometer. I felt
its mercury rolling under my teeth, boiling like language.

A deaf man, an old man, I am his hand, rough and gentle, an arrow here
and then.

Time, I can see what I feel.

In the future even your future becomes my past. Arrow, I have died.
There is peace. I pull it from me like a blanket.

As in a dream, because of time being an arrow, I put on the dress of a
young, lovely mother. Because of her, because of the time, here I am,
always watching over you.

their strange laments beset me,
each an arrow

—Dante Alighieri, *The Inferno,* Canto XXIX

EARTH UNDER GLASS ★ THE CELADON MUSEUM

Tell us again, Father, of the boy who dined lonely on the crush of his own footstep

> No, Children, I will tell you of the black lake of fire to boil the tea of small bodies

> Mother, roast this barley for tea and remind us of the war food and clear spring water

> No, Children, I must remind you of the last dragonfly born on this mountain and why all children need a second throat for when the first is left behind

> Oh Father, sing again of the hidden rims of the body and how old we are here in this time

> Children, once again I ask you to crack this kiln, break this air, crawl into this heated brick box

> Dear Mother, dear Father, we see the light passing through these blackened walls why won't you quench this our first and last thirst

BONGEUNSA TEMPLE, SAMSEONGDONG OF GANGNAMGU DISTRICT

YOU: Slip into space and garland the stone steps.

WE: We came for the Buddha.

YOU: No, we came to see with eyes unclouded with hate.

WE: I came like a shoe for my mate, her rust and retreat.

IT: This pairing flung against the skin head of the painted drum.

ME: A sheaf of rhythm bound me collar and clavicle.

ME: My bad posture made me fetal.

YOU: "The king was no longer considered a Buddha."

US: My posthumous mother, her poetry of obedience shamed my piety.

WE: It's filial, it's heaven, it's the difference between a wife and a concubine.

YOU: The virgin in front of me was my king.

ME: The girl behind me.

YOU: The girl inside me.

US: A goading dictator, a once-again Confucian.

IT: Like the slave girl, let my mortal body fall away.

YOU: Wait for me, wait fast like nightfall, spit on robbers and spirits.

ME: Darken your voice with a deep swallow of stars.

YOU: My life is like a knife in my side.

THE LABOR OF CHILDHOOD

> "The passage of the threshold is a form of self-annihilation."
> Joseph Campbell, *The Hero with a Thousand Faces*

dream, arrival, a fist filled, the tools of one's future—
        ink stamp, coin, horsehair brush.

        This wide and broken orientalia

the milk of one mother, another
toward, face, cut the dictionary like a birthday cake

        a barrel of blueprint rolls, the spindle-leg of compass

a hinge into this day's room, a metal spider walks into the square of day

night by hour, word by syllable as if separating laundry dark from light—until one
earns one's name

to perform the role of the Child with perfection, to skin the costume, one's face in
orbit, reflect light, turn again.

mother and child : boat or bark : acorn and apple-star

"One's costume can be changed."
"One's skin belongs to the clan."
"One's skin belongs to the mother, the mother-skin."
"When a noun becomes a verb, the original noun, something static, is forgotten."
"One's skin belongs to the dictionary."

the labor of the child includes eating one's name, a second or third

it may be digested and it may reappear on the chest as a pin with wings or stars

as clear as a cough, sneeze, or any other spontaneous utterance of the body

we run our hands over our old costumes, the skin now rough and animal, something with which to catch a hot iron

CAMERA OBSCURA

Old light, break up toward this vaulted chamber.
The world made with a breath, an image, this invention.
Hold this room in your hands, corners meet and disappear into points of shadow.
How delightful it is to possess a miniature room filled with dark as if darkness was water.
Hold it too long, the paper will soak and darken, turn soft, collapse, the darkness to leak
everywhere into the world.
The wet, torn box a useless thing, crumpled pulp.
A book of blasphemy, not burned but melted.
Soaked with erased time, my own hands stained with it.
★

Look how he holds his gun just so in front of his face, like a monocle, a microscope, his
scientific eye sighting the enemy down its dull metal barrel.
★

In a dark room full of strangers we watch the image of a man in motion: He is the Hero.
Wasn't he our demigod?
Wasn't he motherless?
I saw that he needs no dark room of the mother holding his skin together.
Hunting. Hunted.
Through a pinprick, into a murky room, exits fore and aft.
The infinity of reproduction.
His gown is made of the time we give him.
Did we see him wounded?

As they grapple, he takes on the stain of enemy blood.
Offer yourself, add to his strength.
He borrows waves of our will to defeat his enemy! We hand him
thing after thing, weapons and time.
Wars of infinity, one by one.

so thick a veil above its currents as this

—DANTE ALIGHIERI, *The Inferno,* Canto XXXII

LABOR OF MEDICINE

I.

Invisible garment forces a body to the floor. *Supplicant, lover, maker of prayers, one by one.* Tear away. Now at the bottom of a boat and alone, salt and sea. Weather of disarray. Feverish dreams of land, the body is dismantled. Collect, rinse, and keep. Where the ocean recedes—like the others, seaweed and a nest of shivers.

II.

The snow is a kind of old medicine, appearing like dying swallows, sharp-tailed, hollow, reduced to a colorless element. At night, a taste of dark pine in the other's mouth. Cut bark, sap, sweet trails bitter. Together to the stand and green and somber while the sharp buds wait for a necklace of white moths. And the sun never has to promise or remember, though all, we all are made of it. Something holds, like sorrow, magnets of grief.

III.

The other, that body hunts. Etiquette, be slain again—all abandoned by manners. Blind back, hear the wind sharpening the aim. Scapula, clavicle. Assemblage in the green-blue alert. Bleached and outlined. Eyes turn and the head follows as if by instinct.

IV.

One day the other grew through, grass waiting in winter. Pale green shoots pinned to lay at hand. Heavy, damp, pierced. Posed the one like Christ and for days the bleeding and the evening dew and the ground grew red beneath. Visitations and visions arrived like weather. Grass buried and mounded. The lamentation, the ignorance. Unanswered. The world forgot—above hung the new bed's canopy, nothing but cloud cover. In transparency, and soon like a sputtering lamp. Overheard an ant colony mocking with industry and floods in miniature. An interrupted prayer. The garden. The dark earth takes its daughter.

V.

Body of the other, bones made of memory. The other looks like a world in surrender. Resembling Christ in a moment of faith, as if lit from within, as if there might be a burning through the fog of night. Eat what is offered. The body brought somewhere safe from the destruction of man. No wristwatch, no man-made music, no apparatus of conversation. No navigation. In fact, no machines of any kind—no future, no aid—may bind tonight.

VI.

Affliction. Chains for the supplicant, a servant-self, superior, past and future. Who has seen this shadow that glitters with beauty, the hardness of no-thought, of no-regret? Clothing thrown on the floor, destroy with dust and gravity. *That one. That other one.* Though the supplicant can be nothing good, steady blur of clockwork or the distraction of a blinded bee. Poison the hum.

VII.

Outside, the other could bend back crown for king. Face the clock
while the black hand shortens the angle, lengthens the hour, cuts the
white of time. Yet other animals keep their clocks inside their blood.
The red hand has traveled—now the sound of keys.

VIII.

Here is the indigo that they eat. Hang cloth and dye you. No one peels
a plum. An apple in love, or its hidden seeds, dusk and star.

IX.

Drawn to the axis, a compass. Solitude of the other. Want of. Sharp plane of streetlamp light. Skim the window shyly, keep a distance.

X.

Boats from a certain tree, a voice runs a length. Not enough to build a house. A shipwright's plane and love. Shining shines. Thin gold is proof and worn down all smooth. Made and used. Mathematical preparations, a rudimentary knowledge of architecture, human bone and muscle. What can and cannot renew itself—a search for this book or that museum, antique ideas. To repair—against the grain, with drunken sails, a stint with toss and pitch.

who pierces the world

—DANTE ALIGHIERI, *The Inferno,* Canto XXXIV

FAMISHED, A BLACK LADDER BLOOD BOX

"woman gravid

CONVENT: MOTHER SURROGATE
PLUNGE INVISIBLE OUTSIDE HISTORY
MAIL THIS COUNTERFEIT WOMB
A BLACK LADDER BLOOD BOX
VOICES AT THE EVENT HORIZON
(IM)PLANT HARVEST TIME VIPER
CONJOIN THIS HOOK AND EYE

with the fertilized egg of another woman"

"our surrogate was amazing

LIBRARIAN FOR A BAKER'S DOZEN
THE ARCHIVES OF RUDYARD KIPLING
VENEER AND FLY BEFORE ME
I CAN INVENT THIS NEW BODY
GARMENT SO COSTLY SO SECRET
FUGITIVE FORGIVE US FILTHY
SWADDLING THIS BLACK CASTE
OPEN YOUR MOUTH HANG MEMORY

though it was hard to give up control"

"she's like an aunt to _____

        INVISIBLE CHILD WHO CAN WEAR IT
        STIRRUPS SADDLE BIT BRIDLE
        AN EXHORTER TO BE HIRED
        YOUR PHOTOGRAPH TO BE HUNG
        SURPLUS REPRODUCTIVE MATERIAL
        NOT TO BE NAMED OR PRESERVED
        UNDER GLASS UNDER TAKEN SUNDER

        I don't get any sleep anymore but I am so in love with
        _____ "

"We went with India,

IT IS GOOD MONEY NOT CHARITY
HEAVEN SHALL LACE ME TIGHT
CLOSE THIS CABINET AND CAVE
CLAIM CHAIN HELIX THE FIX
IT LOOKS JUST LIKE YOU YOU YOU
MIMICRY A FORM OF FLATTERY
FAMISHED FAMILY FAVOR FARM

made the most sense financially; still, it's been a long, costly process"

THE SIBLING LIBRARY

Fill in the name]   [bedraggle

Scat rule of identity

In works   [great learning

          [the first deleted *me* written over

     ★ *Their own or their child's half-siblings, or*
     ★ *their own or their child's sperm or egg donor, or*
     ★ *their own genetic offspring.*

wandering footsteps, soft on the earth

pockets of cakey soil filling with rain

roots and shoots at the co-op

organic fingernails and their carbon aftertaste

                  a multiple, the same child written over and over

rewritten and scattered

And through the bindery
And through the bakery
And through the mortar and pestle and buried jar
And through my own sperm or egg
There. Own.

The name of this donation *We realize, however, that some folks may want to remain anonymous while sharing important medical or genetic information with their fellow "donor families." For these people, we suggest using a throwaway untraceable email address.*

half-name, written over

library of siblings

decentralized nursery, a mobile above the crib

the stars glitter and hang in the placeless blue

A CURIOUS GENEALOGY

virgin births dazzle / dismember / vouch for the reborn / a square
room full of amnesiacs / swimming beneath: an amniotic / around this
table the veneer of the speech of the dead / cover your living face
offends you your hot blush of life / the returned curse the calling /
counterfeiters and clockmakers / spiritualism hoax evil black magic the
veil the vision / a statue has no need for a womb the thick description
of empirical method and beakers and / surgical theater hot white lights
scissors kin division martyr miracle / a statue with oily tears wept and
witnessed / crippled cured raped restored / all disfigurations rewritten
forgiven / a hospital bed was more flexible than my own body / joints
and cranks and pulse / *As I lay dying* / the higher the flag / folded up
in whiteness a letter unsent sharp envelope angles and air / a routine of
exile arrives at limbo / the height of the enemy / my arms open / a
cradle waits sweet pattern of tuck / and double

ENDNOTES

- "... rough // And savage ..." —Dante Alighieri, *The Inferno,* translated by Robert Pinsky, Canto I, line 3–4. (New York: Farrar, Strauss and Giroux, 1994).
- "No sooner were all things ..." —Ovid, *Metamorphoses,* translated by Mary M. Innes. (London: Penguin Books, 1955), 31.
- "All the world's cravings ..." —*The Inferno,* Canto I, line 39
- "Churned in my heart's lake ..." —*The Inferno,* Canto I, line 17
- Fragments in "Best Protect: Clippings" from BBC article "1991: 'Mother of all Battles' Begins," January 17, 1991 http://news.bbc.co.uk/onthisday/hi/dates/stories/january/17 /newsid_2530000/2530375.stm
- "All other loves are masks for these." —*The Inferno,* introduction
- "Away from here ..." —*The Inferno,* Canto I, line 90
- Korean War Maps—U.S. Navy, http://www.koreanwar.org/html/maps_navy.html, Maps from "History of United States Naval Operations: Korea"— Department of the Navy—Navy Historical Center, Washington, DC, http://www.koreanwar.org/html/korean_war_maps_ results_navy .html?map_url=navy_map02
- "Therefore if you escape ..." —*The Inferno,* Canto XVI, line 72
- Central Intelligence Agency Factbook online, entries for South Korea and North Korea, https://www.cia.gov/library/publications /the-world-factbook/
- Fragments of text in the following poems taken from *Korea: 1910* by Angus Hamilton et al.:
  - "My Most Imperfect Knowledge: The 1816 Voyages of the *Alceste* and *Lyra*"
  - "Seoul, December 1883"
  - "1895, The King of Korea Is a Vassal of China"
  - "Coal and Iron and Gold"
  - "American Missionary"

- "August 1950, 8,000 Korean Replacements"
- "Foresight, August 1910"
- "And so I stopped . . ." —*The Inferno,* Canto XIII, line 22
- "Sand kindled like . . ." —*The Inferno,* Canto XIV, line 31
- "Loom, spindle and thimble . . ." —*The Inferno,* Canto XX, 103
- "Their strange laments . . ." —*The Inferno,* Canto XXIX, line 45
- "So thick a veil . . ." —*The Inferno,* Canto XXXII, line 25
- "Who pierces the world . . ." —*The Inferno,* Canto XXXIV, line 107
- Fragments in quotes in "Famished, a Black Ladder Blood Box" from news articles on surrogacy
- In "The Labor of Childhood," quote from Joseph Campbell, *The Hero with a Thousand Faces,* 91
- Italicized lines in "The Sibling Library" from the Donor Sibling Registry, www.donorsiblingregistry.com

ACKNOWLEDGMENTS

I am in debt to Robert Pinsky for his stunning verse translation of *The Inferno*, from which I took the title for this book. Most of the "vestibules" (doorways, entrances, waiting rooms, portals, etc.) throughout *Rough, and Savage* are phrases taken from his *Inferno*.

Another important text in the creation of this book is *Korea: Its History, Its People, and Its Commerce* by Angus Hamilton, Major Herbert II Austin, and Viscount Masatake Terauchi. This book was published in 1910 by J. B. Millet Company, Boston and Tokyo, as Volume XIII of its Oriental Series. The brief introduction to *Korea* is by Percival Lowell of the prominent Boston Lowell family, brother to poet Amy Lowell and A. Lawrence Lowell, a president of Harvard University. During the late 1800s, Percival Lowell was a counselor and foreign secretary to the Korean Special Mission to the United States. He was witness to the fall of Korea as a sovereign entity. In his introduction he writes, "Since the days they feasted me almost all my Korean official friends have met violent deaths. The men I knew are no more, and now the country itself has been wiped from the map. Even as I write, Korea has ceased to exist" (XIV).

Now, in our time, Korea exists, but as a land divided, still officially at war since 1953, and important as an ongoing U.S. interest. According to the United States Forces Korea's pamphlet, the U.S.'s strategic concern in this area of the world is due to its being the "fastest growing part of the global economy, one-fifth of world's economic output"; having "four of the six world's largest militaries"; and representing "twenty-five percent of all U.S. trade."

I am very grateful for the community of fellow poets and writers, friends, family, and Chris Fischbach and everyone at Coffee House Press. Several organizations generously supported the development of this book: the Archibald Bush Foundation, the Minnesota State Arts Board, the Blacklock Nature Sanctuary, the Jerome Foundation, and the Loft Literary Center. *Thank you.*

The poems in this book set in contemporary Korea could not have been written without KEEP (Korean Exposure and Education Program), which is a two-week social justice education and travel program for Korean Americans run by the New York–based nonprofit Nodutdol. Its mission is to bridge divisions created by war, militarism, and social injustice.

I also sincerely thank the dedicated editors of literary journals in which poems and sections of this manuscript first appeared:

"(Naju, Weeding at the Base of the Pear Tree)," *Konundrum Engine Literary Review* (February 2012)

"Isolette," *blink again: sudden fiction from the upper midwest,* eds. John Colburn, Michelle Filkins, and Margaret Miles (2011)

"Beggar } Chooser { Beggar," reassembled from "Which Way | Kichicheon | Yankeetown," *Drunken Boat* 12 (Fall 2010)

"The Sibling Library" as "Donor Sibling Registry," *Water~Stone* (2010)

"Best Protect: Clippings" as "Desert Storm, BBC, 1991," *Rio Grande Review* 33 (Spring 2009)

"Beggar } Chooser { Beggar," reassembled from "Paleolithic Remains," *Little Red Leaves* 3 (2008)

"Bongeunsa Temple, Samseongdong of Gangnamgu District" and "Foresight, August 1910," *Packingtown Review* (Winter 2008)

"(Riot Police); (Pyongtaek, U.S. Military Base Expansion); (Mountain, Jirisan National Park); (Outside the Gate at Camp Humphreys, U.S. Military Base); (Budae Chigae Near the Gi Ji Cheon / "Garbage" Stew Near the Prostitution Camptown)," *Coconut* 11 (2008)

"The Daughter at the Music Stand" as "The Daughter's Semi-Daily Violin Practice," *Cultural Society* (Sep. 2006)

COLOPHON

Rough, and Savage was designed at Coffee House Press, in the historic Grain Belt Brewery's Bottling House near downtown Minneapolis. The text is set in Bembo.

MISSION

The mission of Coffee House Press is to publish exciting, vital, and enduring authors of our time; to delight and inspire readers; to contribute to the cultural life of our community; and to enrich our literary heritage. By building on the best traditions of publishing and the book arts, we produce books that celebrate imagination, innovation in the craft of writing, and the many authentic voices of the American experience.

VISION

LITERATURE. We will promote literature as a vital art form, helping to redefine its role in contemporary life. We will publish authors whose groundbreaking work helps shape the direction of 21st-century literature.

WRITERS. We will foster the careers of our writers by making long-term commitments to their work, allowing them to take risks in form and content.

READERS. Readers of books we publish will experience new perspectives and an expanding intellectual landscape.

PUBLISHING. We will be leaders in developing a sustainable 21st-century model of independent literary publishing, pushing the boundaries of content, form, editing, audience development, and book technologies.

VALUES

Innovation and excellence in all activities

Diversity of people, ideas, and products

Advancing literary knowledge

Community through embracing many cultures

Ethical and highly professional management
and governance practices

Join us in our mission at coffeehousepress.org

FUNDER ACKNOWLEDGMENT

Coffee House Press is an independent nonprofit literary publisher. Our books are made possible through the generous support of grants and gifts from many foundations, corporate giving programs, state and federal support, and through donations from individuals who believe in the transformational power of literature. Coffee House Press receives major operating support from the Bush Foundation, the McKnight Foundation, from Target, and in part from a grant provided by the Minnesota State Arts Board through an appropriation by the Minnesota State Legislature from the state's general fund and its arts and cultural heritage fund with money from the vote of the people of Minnesota on November 4, 2008. Support for this title was received from the National Endowment for the Arts, a federal agency, and through special project support from the Jerome Foundation. Coffee House also receives support from: several anonymous donors; Suzanne Allen; Elmer L. and Eleanor J. Andersen Foundation; Around Town Agency; Patricia Beithon; Bill Berkson; the E. Thomas Binger and Rebecca Rand Fund of the Minneapolis Foundation; the Patrick and Aimee Butler Family Foundation; Ruth Dayton; Dorsey & Whitney, LLP; Mary Ebert and Paul Stembler; Chris Fischbach and Katie Dublinski; Fredrikson & Byron, P.A.; Sally French; Anselm Hollo and Jane Dalrymple-Hollo; Jeffrey Hom; Carl and Heidi Horsch; Alex and Ada Katz; Stephen and Isabel Keating; the Kenneth Koch Literary Estate; Kathy and Dean Koutsky; the Lenfestey Family Foundation; Carol and Aaron Mack; Mary McDermid; Sjur Midness and Briar Andresen; the Rehael Fund of the Minneapolis Foundation; Schwegman, Lundberg & Woessner, P.A.; Kiki Smith; Jeffrey Sugerman; Patricia Tilton; the Archie D. & Bertha H. Walker Foundation; Stu Wilson and Mel Barker; the Woessner Freeman Family Foundation; Margaret and Angus Wurtele; and many other generous individual donors.

ART WORKS.
ARTS.GOV

MINNESOTA
STATE ARTS BOARD

TARGET.

To you and our many readers across the country,
we send our thanks for your continuing support.